180 Days of SOCIAL STUDIES
for Prekindergarten

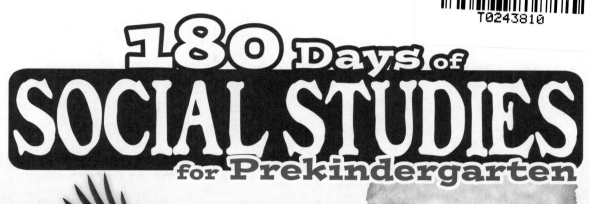

Civics
Economics
Geography
History

Darcy Mellinger, M.A.T., NBCT

Publishing Credits

Corinne Burton, M.A.Ed., *President and Publisher*
Emily R. Smith, M.A.Ed., *SVP of Content Development*
Véronique Bos, *Vice President of Creative*
Lynette Ordoñez, *Content Manager*
Carol Huey-Gatewood, M.A.Ed., *Editor*
Avery Wickersham, *Assistant Editor*
Jill Malcolm, *Graphic Designer*

Standards

Copyright © 2010 National Council for the Social Studies
© 2022 TESOL International Association
© 2022 Board of Regents of the University of Wisconsin System

Image Credits: p.26 (top) Library of Congress [LC-DIG-ppmsca-49864]; p.27 (top) Shutterstock/chrisdorney; p.30 (top) Shutterstock/Tippman98x; p.35 (top) Library of Congress [LC-DIG-det-4a18586], p.38 (bottom left) Shutterstock/Everett Collection; p.39 (bottom) Library of Congress [LC-DIG-ppmsca-12626]; p.43 (top) Shutterstock/thipjang; p.43 (bottom) Shutterstock/PixHound; p.45 (top) Library of Congress [LC-USF34-045684-D]; p.48 (bottom) Shutterstock/Caroline Jane Anderson; p.49 (top) Library of Congress [LC-USZ62-90603]; p.50 (top right) Library of Congress [LC-DIG-fsa-8d25973]; p.51 (top) Library of Congress [LC-DIG-det-4a05674]; p.51 (bottom) Library of Congress [LC-DIG-anrc-12483]; p.52 (top) Library of Congress [LC-DIG-npcc-04400]; p.52 (bottom) Library of Congress [LC-USF34-054238-E]; p.53 (top) Library of Congress [LC-USZ62-26378], p.53 (bottom) Library of Congress [LC-USZ62-39165]; p.60 (top left) Shutterstock/Joseph Sohm; p.63 (top right) Shutterstock/a katz; p.69 (top right) Shutterstock/Jillian Cain Photography; p.147 (top right) Shutterstock/ju_see; p.165 (top center) Shutterstock/Ken Homan; p. 173 (top right) Shutterstock/Aisyaqilumaranas; p.174 (top right) Shutterstock/a katz; p.190 Shutterstock/Turistas; p.193 (top) Shutterstock/Simone Hogan

A division of Teacher Created Materials
5482 Argosy Avenue
Huntington Beach, CA 92649
www.tcmpub.com/shell-education
ISBN 978-1-0876-6266-4
© 2023 Shell Educational Publishing, Inc.
Printed in China
51497

Table of Contents

What Do the Experts Say?

Welcome to *180 Days of Social Studies for Prekindergarten*! The four disciplines of social studies—history, civics, geography, and economics—are introduced and explored in this book. The activities give students practice in the foundational knowledge and analytic skills to understand and make intentional decisions about their world. Through the four disciplines, students come to appreciate and better understand relationships with their families, peers, and communities. Learning becomes more meaningful when students connect their life experiences to social studies concepts.

Foundations

Learning foundational social studies skills will help prepare young students to dive deeper into the content in kindergarten. It is estimated that 85–90 percent of brain growth occurs in the first five years of life (First Things First 2017). Beginning to discuss these meaningful disciplines of history, civics, geography, and economics enriches young minds. In this book, students learn more about themselves and others from diverse backgrounds.

The National Council for the Social Studies (NCSS) recommends that early childhood educators uphold the following principles and approaches in their work with young children:

- Young children have the capacity to use the skills of reasoning and inquiry to investigate social studies concepts as they explore how people interact in the world (Strasser and Bresson 2017). They need multiple and varied opportunities to do this.

- Early childhood is a time when the foundations of social studies are established, and the curriculum should attend to engaging and developing young children's capacity for citizenship, democratic or civic activity, and participation in decision-making, as well as critical disciplinary literacies (NCSS 2010, 2013).

- As you set the tone for children's social studies learning, it is critical that curricular and instructional decisions embrace diversity while intentionally contesting bias and inequity (Durden et al. 2015, Gay 2000, Goodman and Hooks 2016, Ladson-Billings 1995).

By working through this book, young children who are beginning to learn the key ideas in social studies will gain the foundational concepts needed to succeed in elementary school.

What Do the Experts Say? *(cont.)*

The Need for Practice

Through social studies, students begin to understand the world surrounding them and transfer these ideas to new situations. Children learn to discuss their ideas in coherent ways and apply them to social studies concepts, skills, and big ideas. Practice is crucial for students to gain the experiences and confidence to become active citizens in a global society. The activities in this book help students better understand the world they live in at the foundational levels of history, civics, geography, and economics.

Practice Pages

180 Days of Social Studies for Prekindergarten offers a full page of social studies practice for each day of the school year. Every practice page provides content, questions, and activities that are related to social studies topics and standards. These activities introduce and reinforce grade-level skills across a variety of social studies concepts. The content and questions are easy to prepare and implement as part of the daily routine. Regardless of how the pages are used, students will be engaged in practicing the foundational skills to learn social studies through these standards-based activities.

Students are also given the opportunity to extend their learning. Throughout the book, children are encouraged to incorporate the arts into their learning. Students may act, dance, sing, and draw to express their new understandings of social studies concepts. The practice pages in *180 Days of Social Studies for Prekindergarten* are designed to awaken student interest through multiple pathways of experience.

What Do the Experts Say? *(cont.)*

Standards-Based Instruction

The social studies skills included in *180 Days of Social Studies for Prekindergarten* are aligned to standards. (See pages 12–14.) This book is organized in four units based on the social studies disciplines of history, civics, geography, and economics.

In the **History** section, students investigate time, calendars, and holidays. They consider how families lived long ago and compare and contrast this to today. Children also compare and contrast their own educational experiences with those of the past. Finally, students take a historical and current view of communities and neighborhoods.

When students investigate **Civics**, they explore community helpers, citizenship, leaders, rules and responsibilities, and important places in their communities.

In the **Geography** unit, children consider culture as it relates to geography. Students learn what a map is, how to read a map, and how to create a map to demonstrate their learning. Children learn about different land and water forms. They consider different signs and symbols they might find in their communities. Finally, students consider how people live today and long ago as it relates to geography.

Economics can be an abstract concept for children. In the economics section, students learn about the economic concepts of choices, goods and services, money and jobs, and wants and needs.

Diagnostic Assessment

In addition to providing opportunities for frequent practice, you will want to assess student understanding of social studies concepts, big ideas, vocabulary, and reasoning. It is important to effectively address student misconceptions and gaps, build on their current understandings, and challenge their thinking at an appropriate level. Assessment is a long-term process that involves careful analysis of student responses from a multitude of sources. In prekindergarten social studies, this may include classroom discussions, projects, and practice sheets. This book provides a rubric to evaluate student responses on the activities.

How to Use This Book

Using the Practice Pages

The practice pages in this book provide instructional opportunities for each of the 180 days of the school year. Activities are organized into content themes based on the social studies disciplines—history, civics, geography, and economics. Each day's social studies skills are aligned to standards that may be found on pages 12–14 in this book.

Easy-to-follow directions help adults support students as they complete activities.

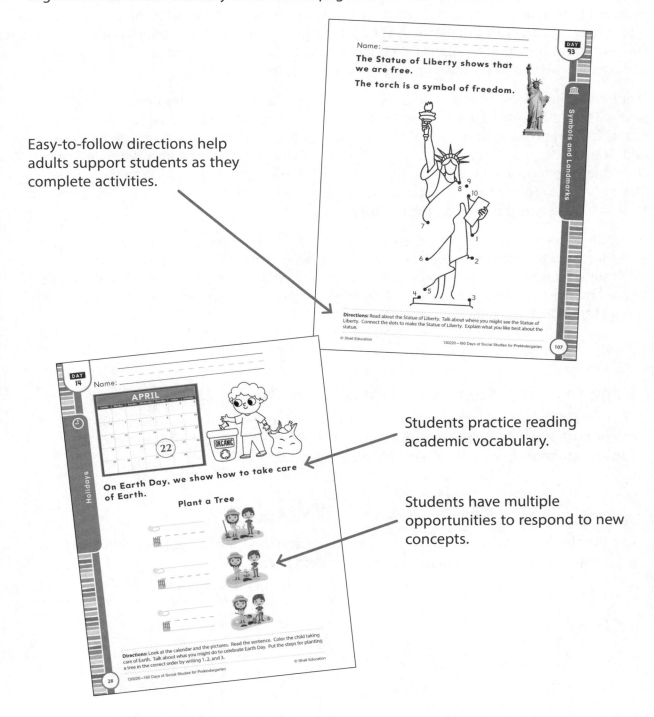

Students practice reading academic vocabulary.

Students have multiple opportunities to respond to new concepts.

How to Use This Book *(cont.)*

Letter Formation and Proper Pencil Grip

When students write throughout the pages of this book, encourage proper pencil grip. It is important for children to learn how to properly grip their pencils early. Students will naturally find their dominant hand. If a student writes with both their right and their left hand, brain research indicates that it is preferred to allow them to write with both hands. The best pencil grip for children is with their pointer finger on the top, thumb on the side, and three fingers below the pencil to support the grip. The grip of the pencil is about one inch from the tip of the pencil. Younger students may have to grow into this grip, so encourage students to try this grip when you see that they are ready.

Aside from the grip, students should also have proper habits and environment in which to write. Teach students to use sharpened pencils. Students should use their nondominant hands to hold down their papers or books. Posture is important, so invite students to sit tall with their backs supported by chairs. Their chairs should be a comfortable distance from the table where they are working. Teach students to press down on pencils with medium strength—not too hard and not too softly. To learn more about this topic, you can check out *How to Hold a Pencil* by Megan Hirsch (2010).

As students trace and write letters, check that they are writing letters accurately. Repetition when learning to write letters will help them later with writing fluency. If students need extra support with their fine-motor skills, you may want to write the letters with highlighters or light markers for students to trace. Examples of all of the uppercase and lowercase letters can be found in the Digital Resources.

Using the "Sky, Fence, and Grass" to Write

There are different ways to write letters. This book suggests forming letters using methods that generally do not require students to lift their pencils off the page. To support students in writing letters, this book has writing.

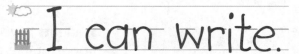

Use the sky, fence, and grass to help students understand how to use the writing lines: sky = top line, fence = midline, and grass = bottom line.

Activities Overview

Over the 180 days of learning, students will examine the basics of history, civics, geography, and economics. The following activities are used throughout this book as students explore social studies topics.

Time to Draw	Students draw pictures to explain what they learned or have experienced related to the topic.
Matching Game	Learners draw lines between related concepts to show matches.
Multiple-Choice Questions	Students circle the better of two choices related to the topic.
Color-by-Code	Children color sections of images based on color-code keys.
Dot-to-Dot	Students connect the dots to make images that support their learning of social studies concepts.
Sequence	Children read steps related to concepts and put the steps in correct, sequential order.
Word Search	Students hunt in word searches to find the academic vocabulary.
Acrostic Poem	Students draw pictures to create acrostic poems to demonstrate what they know about the social studies concepts.

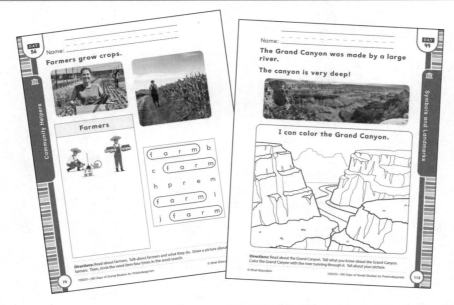

Assessment and Diagnosis

Determine Baseline

When assessing student progress in early childhood, it is important to consider children's developmental levels in all learning domains. Determining each child's or the whole class's baseline can guide instruction in both pacing and depth. You may also want to determine whether a child needs additional support in a content area. When a child or class excels in a content area, it is best to stretch student learning to a higher level of instruction. In that case, you may wish to enrich the learning with additional materials. See the activities in the Digital Resources for ideas to extend and enrich learning.

Progress Monitoring

Formal or diagnostic assessments may be conducted periodically—often once a semester or trimester. You may also prefer to administer pre- and post-assessments. It is excellent practice to assess students at the beginning, middle, and end of the school year. Another way progress may be monitored is at the beginning and end of each of the four disciplines—history, civics, geography, and economics. Teachers and parents are encouraged to collaborate with teams, schools, and other parents to determine what is best for their learners. These formal assessments are used to determine whether a child is thriving with the curriculum or if changes are needed to meet the child's needs.

Assessment and Diagnosis (cont.)

Rubric and Recording Sheets

When analyzing data, it is important for teachers and parents to reflect on how their teaching practices influenced students' responses and to identify areas where additional instruction may be needed. Essentially, the data gathered from assessments will be used to inform instruction: to slow down, to continue as planned, to speed up, or to reteach in a new way.

You may use the practice pages as formative assessments of the key social studies disciplines. The rubric and recording pages included in this book allow you to quickly score students' work and monitor their progress on the written response assignments. (See pages 196–199 in this book and the Digital Resources.) The answer key on pages 201–207 provides answers for the written, matching, and multiple-choice response questions. The rubric may be used for any open-ended questions where student responses vary.

It is developmentally appropriate at this level for a child to express ideas with drawings only. It may be helpful to review the Stages of Emergent Writing (Byington and Kim 2017) to analyze and track student progress. In these cases, you will want to discuss the child's written response to ensure you understand what the child was expressing in their drawings.

After the last day of practice (Day 180), you may use the certificate on page 195 or in the Digital Resources to celebrate students' learning achievements.

Standards Correlations

Shell Education is committed to producing educational materials that are research and standards based. To support this effort, this resource is correlated to the academic standards of all 50 states, the District of Columbia, the Department of Defense Dependent Schools, and the Canadian provinces. A correlation is also provided for key professional educational organizations.

To print a customized correlation report for your state, please visit our website at **www.tcmpub.com/administrators/correlations** and follow the online directions. If you require assistance in printing correlation reports, please contact the Customer Service Department at 1-800-858-7339.

NCSS Standards and the C3 Framework

The activities in this book are aligned to the following National Council for the Social Studies (NCSS) standards and the C3 Framework.

Discipline	Social Studies Topic	NCSS Theme
History	Time and Calendars	**Change, Continuity, and Context** • Create a chronological sequence of multiple events.
	Holidays	**Change, Continuity, and Context** • Create a chronological sequence of multiple events.
	Families Then and Now	**Change, Continuity, and Context** • Compare life in the past to life today. **Perspectives** • Compare perspectives of people in the past to those of people in the present.
	Schools Then and Now	**Change, Continuity, and Context** • Compare life in the past to life today. **Perspectives** • Compare perspectives of people in the past to those of people in the present.
	Communities and Neighborhoods	**Change, Continuity, and Context** • Generate questions about individuals and groups who have shaped a significant historical change.
Civics	Community Helpers	**Civic and Political Institutions** • Explain how all people, not just official leaders, play important roles in a community.
	Citizenship	**Civic and Political Institutions** • Explain how all people, not just official leaders, play important roles in a community.

Standards Correlations (cont.)

Discipline	Social Studies Topic	NCSS Theme
Civics	Citizenship	**Participation and Deliberation: Applying Civic Virtues and Democratic Principles** • Apply civic virtues when participating in school settings. • Describe democratic principles such as equality, fairness, and respect for legitimate authority and rules. **Processes, Rules, and Laws** • Explain how people can work together to make decisions in the classroom. • Identify and explain how rules function in public (classroom and school) settings.
Civics	Leaders	**Civic and Political Institutions** • Describe roles and responsibilities of people in authority. • Explain what governments are and some of their functions.
Civics	Rules and Responsibility	**Civic and Political Institutions** • Explain the need for and purposes of rules in various settings inside and outside of school. • Describe how communities work to accomplish common tasks, establish responsibilities, and fulfill roles of authority. **Processes, Rules, and Laws** • Explain how people can work together to make decisions in the classroom. • Identify and explain how rules function in public (classroom and school) settings.
Civics	Symbols and Landmarks	**History: Change, Continuity, and Context** • Generate questions about individuals and groups who have shaped a significant historical change.
Geography	Culture	**Human-Environment Interaction: Place, Regions, and Culture** • Explain how weather, climate, and other environmental characteristics affect people's lives in a place or region.
Geography	Maps and Geography	**Geographic Representations: Spatial Views of the World** • Construct maps, graphs, and other representations of familiar places. • Use maps, graphs, photographs, and other representations to describe places and the relationships and interactions that shape them. • Use maps, globes, and other simple geographic models to identify cultural and environmental characteristics of places.
Geography	Signs and Symbols	**Geographic Representations: Spatial Views of the World** • Use maps, globes, and other simple geographic models to identify cultural and environmental characteristics of places.

Standards Correlations (cont.)

Discipline	Social Studies Topic	NCSS Theme
Geography	How People Live	**Human-Environment Interaction: Place, Regions, and Culture** • Explain how weather, climate, and other environmental characteristics affect people's lives in a place or region. **Human-Environment Interaction: Place, Regions, and Culture** • Describe how human activities affect the cultural and environmental characteristics of places or regions. • Identify some cultural and environmental characteristics of specific places.
Economics	Choices	**Economic Decision Making** • Explain how scarcity necessitates decision-making. • Identify the benefits and costs of making various personal decisions. **Exchange and Markets** • Describe examples of costs of production. **The National Economy** • Explain why people save.
	Goods and Services	**Exchange and Markets** • Describe the skills and knowledge required to produce certain goods and services. • Describe the goods and services that people in the local community produce and those that are produced in other communities. • Identify prices of products in a local market. **The National Economy** • Describe examples of capital goods and human capital.
	Money and Jobs	**Exchange and Markets** • Explain how people earn income. **The National Economy** • Describe examples of capital goods and human capital.
	Needs and Wants	**Economic Decision Making** • Explain how scarcity necessitates decision-making. • Identify the benefits and costs of making various personal decisions.

TESOL and WIDA Standards

In this book, the following English language development standard is met: Standard 1: English language learners communicate for social and instructional purposes within the school setting.

Name: _____

Today is the present day.

Time to Draw

This is what I did today.

Directions: Read about and trace the word *today*. Talk about what you have already done today. Draw a picture of it. Talk about what else you might do today.

Name: _____

Tomorrow is the day after today.

Time to Draw

What will I do tomorrow?

Directions: Read about and trace the word *tomorrow*. Talk about what you want to do tomorrow. Draw a picture of it. Tell about your picture.

Name: _____

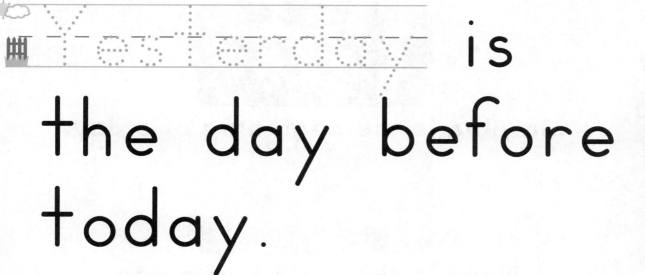

Yesterday is the day before today.

Time to Draw

What did I do yesterday?

Directions: Read about and trace the word *yesterday*. Talk about what you did yesterday. Draw a picture of it. Tell about your picture.

Name: _____

Morning is the beginning of a day.

Noon is the middle of a day.

Night is the time after sunset.

Time to Draw

Morning	Noon	Night

Directions: Read about morning, noon, and night. Talk about what you do in the morning, at noon, and at night. Draw what you like to do each time of day. Share your pictures.

Name: _____

Sunday	Monday	Tuesday	Wednesday	Thursday	Friday	Saturday

Time to Draw

My favorite day is

_____

------------------------ .

Directions: Talk about the days of the week. Read the sentence, and write your favorite day of the week. Draw what you like to do on that day. Tell someone why this is your favorite day.

Name: _____

Sunday	Monday	Tuesday	Wednesday	Thursday	Friday	Saturday

Time and Calendars

Time to Draw

On the weekend I like to _____ .

Directions: Talk about the days of the week and how Saturday and Sunday are called the *weekend*. Read the sentence. Write what you like to do on the weekend. Draw a picture about the weekend. Tell about your picture.

Name: _____

January 1	February 2	March 3	April 4	May 5	June 6
July 7	August 8	September 9	October 10	November 11	December 12

1. Which is a cold winter day?

2. Which should you wear on a cold winter day?

Directions: Talk about the 12 months of the year. Look at the pictures in the winter months of December, January, and February. Talk about what you like to do outside in the winter. Circle the pictures that answer the questions.

Name: _____

January 1	February 2	March 3	April 4	May 5	June 6
July 7	August 8	September 9	October 10	November 11	December 12

Time to Draw

This is spring.

Directions: Talk about the 12 months of the year. Look at the pictures in the spring months of March, April, and May. Read the sentence. Trace the word *spring*. Draw yourself in the spring. Talk about what you enjoy doing in the spring.

Name: _____

January 1	February 2	March 3	April 4	May 5	June 6
July 7	August 8	September 9	October 10	November 11	December 12

| red | tan | blue | yellow |

Directions: Talk about the 12 months of the year. Look at the pictures in the summer months of June, July, and August. Talk about where you like to go in the summer. Use the color code to color the picture.

Name: _____

January 1	February 2	March 3	April 4	May 5	June 6
July 7	August 8	September 9	October 10	November 11	December 12

Time to Draw

This is fall.

Directions: Talk about the 12 months of the year. Look at the pictures in the fall months of September, October, and November. Read the sentence. Trace the word *fall*. Draw yourself in the fall. Talk about what you like to do in the fall.

Name: _____

DECEMBER

Sunday	Monday	Tuesday	Wednesday	Thursday	Friday	Saturday
		1	2	3	4	5	6
7	8	9	10	11	12	13
14	15	16	17	18	19	20
21	22	23	24	25	26	27
28	29	30 New Year's Eve	31 New Year's Day			

Holidays

Time to Draw

New Year's Day

Directions: Look at the calendar and the pictures. Talk about New Year's Eve and New Year's Day. Trace *New Year's Day*. Draw how you celebrate it. Tell about your picture.

Name: _____

JANUARY						
Sunday	Monday	Tuesday	Wednesday	Thursday	Friday	Saturday
				1	2	3
4	5	6	7	8	9	10
11	12	13	14	15	16	17
18	Martin Luther King Jr. Day 19	20	21	22	23	24
25	26	27	28	29	30	31

Martin Luther King Jr. taught that people should be treated fairly.

We think of him on this day.

Time to Draw

Directions: Look at the calendar and the picture. Read about Martin Luther King Jr. Talk about what you might do to celebrate on this day. Draw what you might do on Martin Luther King Jr. Day. Talk about how you can treat people fairly.

26   130220—180 Days of Social Studies for Prekindergarten   © Shell Education

Name: _____

FEBRUARY						
Sunday	Monday	Tuesday	Wednesday	Thursday	Friday	Saturday
	1	2	3	4	5	6
7	8	9	10	11	12	13
14	15 Presidents' Day	16	17	18	19	20
21	22	23	24	25	26	27
28						

Presidents' Day celebrates the first president, George Washington.

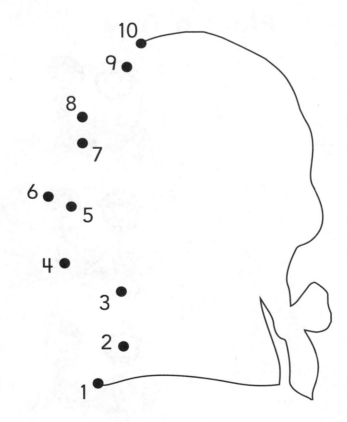

Directions: Look at the calendar and the pictures. Read the text. Talk about why people might celebrate Presidents' Day. Connect the dots to make George Washington. Color the picture.

Holidays

Name: _____

APRIL						
Sunday	Monday	Tuesday	Wednesday	Thursday	Friday	Saturday
				1	2	3
14	5	6	7	8	9	10
11	12	13	14	15	16	17
18	19	20	21	**22**	23	24
25	26	27	28	29	30	

On Earth Day, we show how to take care of Earth.

Plant a Tree

Directions: Look at the calendar and the pictures. Read the sentence. Color the child taking care of Earth. Talk about what you might do to celebrate Earth Day. Put the steps for planting a tree in the correct order by writing 1, 2, and 3.

Name: _____

MAY						
Sunday	Monday	Tuesday	Wednesday	Thursday	Friday	Saturday
			1	2	3	4	5
6	7	8	9	10	11	12
13	14	15	16	17	18	19
20	21	22	23	24	25	26
27 Memorial Day	29	30	31			

On Memorial Day, we remember people who have kept our country safe.

Time to Draw

Directions: Look at the calendar and the pictures. Read the text. Draw a Memorial Day parade. Include an American flag. Tell about your picture.

Holidays

Name: _____

On Juneteenth, people celebrate freedom.

1	2	3	4
yellow	red	blue	green

Directions: Look at the calendar and the pictures. Read the text. Use the color code to color the picture.

130220—180 Days of Social Studies for Prekindergarten   © Shell Education

Name: _____

★ ▅ ★ JULY ★ ▅ ★						
Sunday	Monday	Tuesday	Wednesday	Thursday	Friday	Saturday
				1	2	3
4	5	6	7	8	9	10
11	12	13	14	15	16	17
18	19	20	21	22	23	24
25	26	27	28	29	30	31

Time to Draw

b (J u l y)

b a e f c

J u l y d

g J u l y

J u l y h

Directions: Look at the calendar and the pictures. Talk about what you might do to celebrate on this day. Circle the word *July* four times in the word search. Then, draw how you might celebrate Independence Day. Tell about your picture.

Holidays

Name: _____

SEPTEMBER						
Sunday	Monday	Tuesday	Wednesday	Thursday	Friday	Saturday
				1	2	3
	Labor Day 5	6	7	8	9	10
11	12	13	14	15	16	17
18	19	20	21	22	23	24
25	26	27	28	29	30	

Labor Day is a holiday to celebrate workers.

Many people get this day off from work.

Time to Draw

Directions: Look at the calendar and the pictures. Read about Labor Day. Talk about what you might do to celebrate on this day. Draw a worker who you can celebrate on Labor Day. Talk about the person and how you can celebrate them.

Name: _____

Holidays

On Veterans Day, we thank people who help keep our country safe.

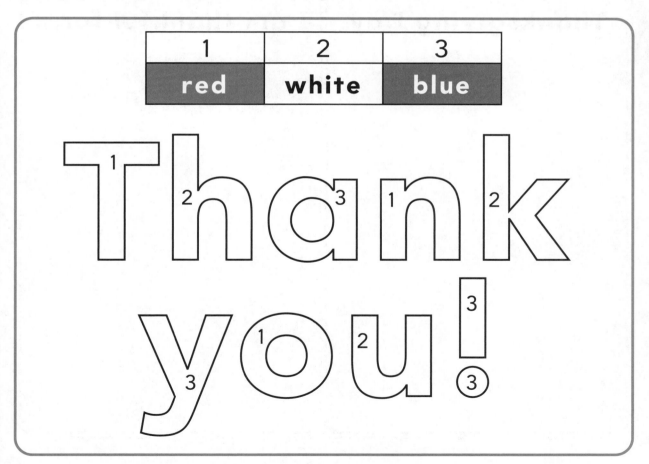

1	2	3
red	white	blue

Directions: Look at the calendar and the pictures. Read about Veterans Day. Talk about who veterans are. Use the color code to color the words *thank you*.

Name: _____

Holidays

NOVEMBER						
Sunday	Monday	Tuesday	Wednesday	Thursday	Friday	Saturday
		1	2	3	4	5
6	7	8	9	10	11	12
13	14	15	16	17	18	19
20	21	22	23 Thanksgiving	24	25	26
27	28	29	30			

Time to Draw

Thanksgiving Day	I am thankful for...

Directions: Look at the calendar and the pictures. Talk about what you might do to celebrate on this day. Draw how you celebrate on Thanksgiving Day. Draw something you are thankful for. Tell about your pictures.

long ago

apartment

long ago

house

today

homestead

today

apartment

Families Then and Now

Directions: Look at the examples of homes from long ago and from today. Talk about what you see. Draw lines to show which homes are from long ago and which are from today.

Name: _____

Families Then and Now

(Time to Draw)

Directions: Look at the examples of how people get their food. Talk about what you see. Label one image as *then*. Label the other image as *now*. Draw one way you get your food today.

Name: _____

Then	Now
 river	 drinking fountain
 well	
 pump	

Directions: Look at the examples of how people got their water long ago. Talk about what you see and how people get their water today. Draw how you get your water. Tell about your picture.

Name: _____

knitting

factory

sewing at home

knitting

factory

sewing at home

Directions: Look at the examples of how people made their clothing long ago and today. Talk about what you see. Circle the examples from long ago with blue and the examples from today with red.

Families Then and Now

Name: _____

Then	Now
walking	
riding	
floating	

Directions: Look at the examples of how people traveled long ago. Talk about what you see and how people travel today. Draw how you travel today. Tell about your picture.

Name: _____

Then	Now
mail	
telephone	
computer	

Directions: Look at the examples of how people communicated long ago. Talk about what communication means and how people communicate today. Draw how you communicate today. Tell about your picture.

Name: _____

Time to Draw

How do you make light today?

1. Which shows a way to make light today?

2. Which shows a way to make light long ago?

Directions: Talk about what you see and how people make light today. Draw how you make light today. Tell about your picture. Then, read the questions and circle the best answers.

Name: _____

Families Then and Now

Then	Now
feather quill	
chalk	

Directions: Look at the examples of tools people used to write with long ago. Talk about what you see and what people use to write with today. Draw how you write today. Tell about your picture.

Then	Now
 painting  drawing  pottery	

Directions: Look at the examples of how people made art long ago. Talk about what you see and how people make art today. Draw how you make art. Tell about your picture.

Name: _____

Families Then and Now

long ago

plastic figures

long ago

corn husk dolls

today

wooden games

today

video games

Directions: Look at the examples of toys from long ago and from today. Talk about what you see. Draw lines to show which toys are from long ago and which are from today.

Name: _____

Then	Now
walking	
riding	

Directions: Look at the examples of children going to school long ago. Talk about what you see. Draw how you get to school today. Tell about your picture.

Name: _____

Then	Now
 one-room schoolhouse	

Directions: Look at the example of a school from long ago. Talk about what you see. Draw where you learn today. Tell about your picture. Connect the dots to make a school from long ago.

Name: _____

Then	Now
 students of all ages	
students of all ages	

Directions: Look at the examples of students in schools long ago. Talk about what you see. Draw who you learn with today. Tell about your picture.

Name: _____

Then	Now
 desks	
 benches	

Directions: Look at the examples of where students learned long ago. Talk about what you see. Draw where you learn today. Tell about your picture.

Then	Now
chalkboard	
chalkboard	

Directions: Look at the examples of boards from schools long ago. Talk about what you see. Draw what boards look like today. Tell about your picture.

Name: _____

Schools Then and Now

Time to Draw

Directions: Look at the examples of how students dressed over time. Talk about what you see. Draw how students dress today. Tell about your picture.

Name: _____

Then	Now
 lunch baskets	
lunch tins	

Directions: Look at the examples of how children carried their lunch long ago. Talk about what you see. Draw what lunchtime looks like for you today. Tell about your picture.

Schools Then and Now

Name: _____

Then	Now
 baseball	
 marbles	

z	p	l	a	y
b	a	e	x	w
p	l	a	y	d
g	p	l	a	y
p	l	a	y	h

Directions: Look at the examples of how children played long ago. Talk about what you see. Draw what you play with your friends. Tell about your picture. Then, circle the word *play* four times in the word search.

Name: _____

Then	Now
 no talking in class	
 sit up straight	

Directions: Look at the examples of class rules long ago. Talk about what you see. Draw a picture showing a rule where you learn today. Tell about your picture.

DAY 40

Schools Then and Now

Name: _____

books

chalkboards

computers

books

markers

Time to Draw

Directions: Look at the examples of learning tools from long ago and from today. Talk about what you see. Draw the tools you use to learn.

Name: _____

Communities are groups of people.

They live and work together.

They play and learn together.

Time to Draw

Directions: Read about communities. Look at the examples of communities. Talk about the kinds of communities you are a part of. Draw your communities.

Name: _____

shoemaking
(cobbler)

plowing (farmer)

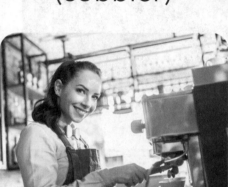

making coffee
(barista)

flying airplanes (pilot)

Time to Draw

construction

Directions: Look at the examples of work from long ago and from today. Talk about what you see. Draw what people do for work in your community.

Name: _____

Communities celebrate

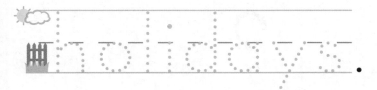
holidays.

Time to Draw

Directions: Read the sentence. Trace the word *holidays*. Talk about the holidays you celebrate in your community and with your family. Draw pictures of these holidays. Tell about your pictures.

Name: _____

How do you celebrate

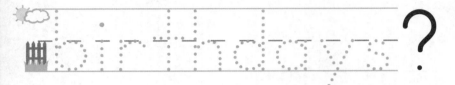

birthdays?

Communities and Neighborhoods

Directions: Read the question. Trace the word *birthdays*. Talk about the way you celebrate birthdays with your family and community. Circle the pictures of people celebrating birthdays.

Name: _____

Time to Draw

Other Celebrations

Directions: Read the heading, and look at the pictures. Talk about the ways you celebrate weddings, parties, or other special days with your family and community. Draw how you celebrate one of these special occasions. Tell about your picture.

Name: _____

Time to Draw

How do you celebrate sports?

1. Which shows a way to play sports?

2. Which shows a way to celebrate sports?

Directions: Read the question. Look at the examples. Talk about the ways you play or celebrate sports. Tell about your picture. Circle the best picture to answer each question.

Name: _____

How do you celebrate the arts?

Time to Draw

Art	Music

Directions: Read the question. Talk about the ways you celebrate the arts with your family and community. Draw how you celebrate art and music. Tell about your pictures.

Name: _____

Neighborhoods are where people live by one another.

Time to Draw

Directions: Read the sentence. Look at the examples of neighborhoods. Talk about your neighborhood. Draw the homes and neighbors that are nearest to you. Explain what you like about your neighborhood.

130220—180 Days of Social Studies for Prekindergarten

Neighborhood Celebrations

Time to Draw

Directions: Talk about the way you celebrate, or would like to celebrate, with your neighbors. Draw a picture to show what you talked about.

Communities and Neighborhoods

Name: _____

You can help in your neighborhood.

Time to Draw

Directions: Read the sentence. Look at the examples of ways to help in a neighborhood. Draw how you help, or would like to help, in your neighborhood. Tell about your picture.

Name: _____

Firefighters put out fires.

Firefighting Tools	Firefighters in My Community

Directions: Read about firefighters. Color the firefighting tools. Talk about firefighters in your community. Draw a picture of firefighters. Explain what you know about the job of fighting fires.

Name: _____

Police officers help keep us safe.

Directions: Read about police officers. Talk about police officers in your community. Connect the dots, and color the picture.

Name: _____

A trash collector takes people's trash.

Trash Collectors	Trash-Collecting Tools

Directions: Read about trash collectors. Talk about trash collectors in your community. Then, color the tools trash collectors use to work. Explain what you know about trash-collecting tools.

Name: _____

Lifeguards keep swimmers safe.

Lifeguards	Lifeguard Tools
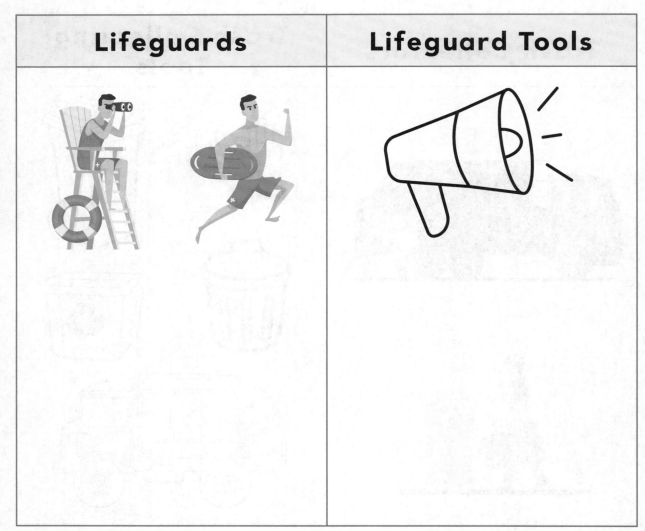	

Directions: Read about lifeguards. Talk about lifeguards in your community. Draw a picture about lifeguards. Then, draw tools that lifeguards need to work. Explain what you know about tools that lifeguards use.

Name: _____

Mail carriers deliver mail.

Mailing a Letter

Directions: Read about mail carriers. Talk about mail carriers in your community. Put the steps for mailing a letter in the correct order by writing 1, 2, and 3.

Name: _____

Farmers grow crops.

Farmers

f	a	r	m	b
c	f	a	r	m
h	p	r	e	m
f	a	r	m	l
j	f	a	r	m

Directions: Read about farmers. Talk about farmers and what they do. Draw a picture about farmers. Then, circle the word *farm* four times in the word search.

Name: _____

A Teacher helps students learn.

Teachers

Directions: Read about teachers. Talk about teachers in your community. Draw a picture about teachers. Explain what you know about teachers.

Name: _____

Healthcare workers help people take care of their bodies.

Healthcare Workers

Directions: Read about healthcare workers. Talk about healthcare workers in your community. Color the examples. Tell about these pictures.

130220—180 Days of Social Studies for Prekindergarten   © Shell Education

Name: _____

Utility workers help people with utilities.

Utilities are things such as water, light, air conditioning, and heat.

Utility Workers	Utility Worker Tools
	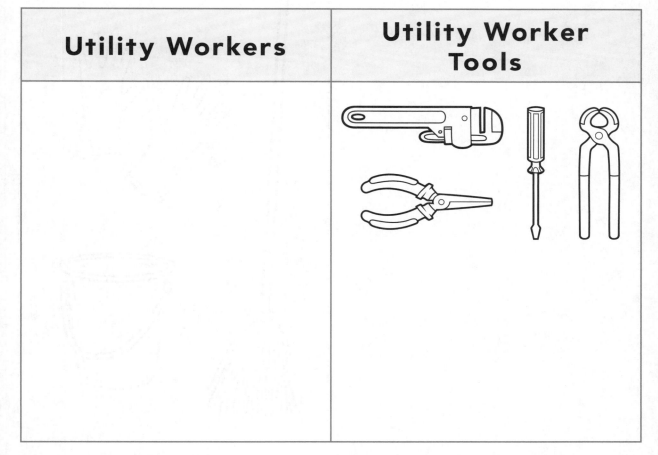

Directions: Read about utility workers. Talk about utility workers in your community. Draw a picture of a utility worker. Then, color the examples of tools that utility workers need to work. Draw one more tool. Explain what you know about these tools.

Name: _____

Custodians keep buildings safe and clean.

Custodians	Custodian Tools

Directions: Read about custodians. Talk about what custodians do. Draw a picture of custodians. Then, color the examples of tools custodians use. Talk about these tools.

130220—180 Days of Social Studies for Prekindergarten

Name: _____

Good citizens are polite.

Time to Draw

Being Polite at Home

Directions: Read about and trace the word *polite*. Color the examples of being polite. Talk about being polite. Draw a picture about being polite at home. Act out being polite.

Citizenship

Name: _____

Honesty means telling the truth.

I broke it.

Time to Draw

Directions: Read about and trace the word *honesty.* Color the example. Talk about being honest. Draw a picture about being honest. Act out being honest.

Name: _____

Fairness means treating people equally.

We each get one!

fair

unfair

fair

Directions: Read about fairness. Color the example. Talk about fairness. Look at the pictures of people being fair and unfair. Draw a line from each word to a picture that matches.

Citizenship

Name: _____

Responsibility means you do the things you are supposed to do.

Time to Draw

How can I be responsible?

Directions: Read about responsibility. Read the question. Color the examples. Talk about responsibility. Draw a picture about being responsible. Act out being responsible.

Name: _____

Respect means honoring people.

Showing Respect

Directions: Read about respect. Look at the example. Talk about showing respect. Circle the pictures of children showing respect. Color those pictures. Act out one of the pictures that shows respect.

Name: _____

Cooperation means working with others.

Let's do this together.

Time to Draw

How can I cooperate?

Directions: Read about cooperation. Look at the examples of cooperation. Talk about cooperation. Draw a picture of people cooperating. Act out cooperating .

Sharing means giving to others.

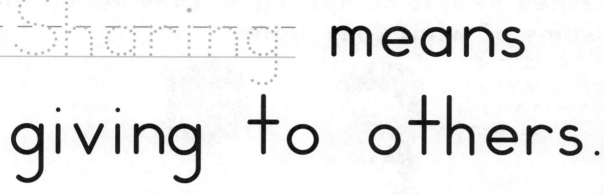

Citizenship

1. Which shows sharing?

2. Which shows a better way to share?

Directions: Read about and trace the word *sharing*. Look at the example. Talk about sharing. Act out sharing. Circle the pictures that best answer the questions.

Citizenship

Name: _____

When people compromise, they each get some of what they want.

Directions: Read about compromise. Talk about how people compromise at home or in your community. Color the pictures that show compromise. Act out compromising.

130220—180 Days of Social Studies for Prekindergarten

Name: _____

A conflict is a problem.

It can happen when people do not agree.

They might argue.

They can talk to solve the conflict.

Solving a Conflict

1	2	3	4
brown	yellow	blue	green

Directions: Read about conflict. Talk about solving a conflict. Use the color code to color the picture. Act out talking to solve a conflict.

Name: _____

People make choices about what they want.

Time to Draw

I Make Choices

Directions: Read about choices. Talk about choices you make at home and in your community. Draw a picture about making choices. Act out making choices.

Name: _____

Leaders guide other people.

They work with others.

Time to Draw

Who is a leader?

Directions: Read about leaders. Color the examples of leaders. Draw a picture of a leader you know. Act out being a leader.

Leaders

Name: _____

A follower follows a leader.

Follow the Leader

Directions: Read about followers. Talk about followers where you learn. Act out following a leader. Connect the dots to make a picture about following. Color the picture.

Name: _____

A leader sets a good example.

Time to Draw

What are leaders like?

Leaders are honest.

I broke it.

Leaders make choices.

Leaders work with others.

Directions: Read about leaders. Draw pictures to show making choices and working with others. Talk about leaders in your community who work with others.

Name: _____

Leaders know their talents and have ideas to try.

I am good at sharing.

Time to Draw

My Talents	I have good ideas.

Directions: Read about leaders. Talk about how you are a leader. Draw your talents and ideas. Act out showing leadership.

Leaders

Name: _____

Leaders

are honest	have ideas
 I broke it.	 I am good at sharing.

use their talents	make choices

work with others

Let's do this together.

Directions: Read about leaders. Talk about leaders. Color the examples.

Name: _____

Leaders

Time to Draw

Who are leaders where you learn?

Directions: Read the question. Talk about leaders where you learn. Draw the leaders where you learn. Tell about your picture.

130220—180 Days of Social Studies for Prekindergarten

© Shell Education

Time to Draw

Who are leaders in your town?

Directions: Talk about leaders. Color the examples. Read the question. Talk about leaders in your town. Draw a picture about leaders in your town. Tell about your picture.

Name: _____

Who is being a leader?

I broke it.

Directions: Read the question. Review Day 75 about leaders. Circle three examples of students being leaders. Explain how students are being leaders. Color the pictures.

130220—180 Days of Social Studies for Prekindergarten

© Shell Education

Name: _____

You can be a leader at home.

Time to Draw

What will you add for the birthday party?

Directions: Read the sentence. Talk about the examples of being a leader at home. Read the question. Be a leader. Use your good ideas to draw things for a birthday party at home. Talk about your ideas for a birthday party at home. Color the picture.

Name: _____

Leaders

You can be a leader.

honesty	ideas	talents	choices	working with others
yellow	pink	orange	red	purple

Directions: Read the sentence and the signs. Talk about how you can be a leader. Use the color code to color the signs and the kids. Add yourself to the picture.

Name: _____

Rules help us keep order and be safe.

No running.

Time to Draw

What rules do I know?	

How are rules made?

Class Rules

Directions: Read about and trace the word *rules*. Read the questions. Talk about rules you know and how rules are made. Draw a picture of rules you know. Circle the pictures that show how rules are made.

Name: _____

Rules help us keep order and be safe.

Time to Draw

Why do we need rules?

STOP

Directions: Read about rules. Look at the examples. Read the question and color the examples. Talk about why rules are needed. Draw a picture about why rules are needed. Tell about your picture.

Name: _____

Rules help us keep order and be safe.

rule at a park

rule on a street

rule at a store

rule in a home

Directions: Read about rules. Talk about rules where you live. Draw lines from the words to the matching examples of rules where you live. Color the examples.

Name: _____

Rules help us keep order and be safe.

Rules Where You Learn

Directions: Read about rules. Talk about rules where you learn. Circle the examples of children following school rules. Act out the rules.

Rules and Responsibilities

Name: _____

Who is following the rules?

Time to Draw

Directions: Read the question. Talk about the rules you see the children following. Circle the examples of children who are following the rules. Draw yourself following a rule. Tell about your picture.

Name: _____

Laws are official rules in a state or country.

Time to Draw

What are laws?

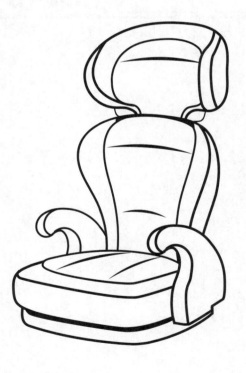

Directions: Read about laws. Talk about laws and the laws you follow. Color the examples of laws. Draw yourself in the car seat. Explain how a car seat keeps you safe.

Name: _____

Laws help keep us safe.

Directions: Read about laws. Talk about how laws help keep us safe. Draw yourself putting trash in the trash bin. Explain how this can help keep you safe. Color the examples of laws that help keep us safe.

Name: _____

Rules help us keep order and be safe.

Laws are official rules in a state or country.

Directions: Read about rules and laws. Talk about how rules and laws are different. Circle the rules. Talk about the rules you circled.

Name: _____

Why should we follow rules?

Time to Draw

Rules help us have fun and be safe.

Directions: Talk about why rules should be followed. Draw a picture of you and your friends following a rule. Act out the rule that you are following.

Rules and Responsibilities

Name: _____

Why should we follow laws?

Time to Draw

Laws help us keep order and be safe.

Directions: Read the question. Talk about what might happen when laws are not followed. Read about laws. Complete the picture by showing the family walking the dog with a leash. Explain how a leash helps keep the family and the dog safe.

Name: _____

The American flag is red, white, and blue.

It has 50 white stars.

There are 13 red and white stripes on the flag.

Time to Draw

American Flag

Directions: Read about the American flag. Talk about where there are American flags in your community. Color the example of the American flag. Draw a picture about the American flag. Tell about your picture.

Symbols and Landmarks

Name: _____

The bald eagle is a symbol of America.

It is strong and free.

Why is the bald eagle a symbol?

It helps us think about being strong and free.

I can draw an eagle.

Directions: Read about the bald eagle. Talk about where you might see a bald eagle. Read about symbols. Connect the dots to make a bald eagle. Color the bald eagle.

130220—180 Days of Social Studies for Prekindergarten

Name: _____

The Statue of Liberty shows that we are free.

The torch is a symbol of freedom.

Directions: Read about the Statue of Liberty. Talk about where you might see the Statue of Liberty. Connect the dots to make the Statue of Liberty. Explain what you like best about the statue.

Name: _____

The Washington Monument is very tall.
It helps us remember George Washington.
He was our first president.

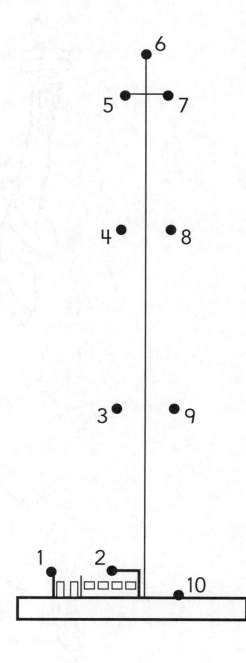

Directions: Read about the Washington Monument. Color the dollar bill. Talk about George Washington and the monument. Connect the dots to make the Washington Monument.

Name: _____

Mount Rushmore is a landmark.

It shows the faces of four presidents.

One of them is George Washington.

Mount Rushmore

Directions: Read about Mount Rushmore. Explain what you know about Mount Rushmore. Color Mount Rushmore in red, white, and blue to represent America.

Symbols and Landmarks

Name: _____

The White House is where the president lives and works.

It is in Washington, DC.

I can draw the White House.

Directions: Read about the White House. Tell what you know about the White House. Trace the lines to draw the White House. Talk about the shapes you see.

Name: _____

The Lincoln Memorial is a landmark.

It helps us remember Abraham Lincoln.

He was a president.

Time to Draw

Abraham Lincoln

b	j	A	b	e
b	a	l	m	n
A	b	e	y	d
g	k	A	b	e
A	b	e	q	t

Directions: Read about the Lincoln Memorial. Tell what you know about the Lincoln Memorial. Draw a picture of Abraham Lincoln. Then, circle the word *Abe* four times in the word search.

Name: _____

This is a home called a pueblo.
You can see it in Colorado.

This is the Taos Pueblo.
People still live in this pueblo.

Directions: Read about Mesa Verde National Park. Look at the very old pueblo. Talk about what you see. Read about Taos Pueblo. Look at the picture of the pueblo from today. Talk about how the pueblos are the same and different.

Name: _____

The Grand Canyon was made by a large river.

The canyon is very deep!

I can color the Grand Canyon.

Directions: Read about the Grand Canyon. Tell what you know about the Grand Canyon. Color the Grand Canyon with the river running through it. Tell about your picture.

Symbols and Landmarks

Name: _____

Old Faithful is a geyser.

Steam shoots up from the ground.

People come to watch this geyser.

Time to Draw

Old Faithful

What is a geyser?

Directions: Read about Old Faithful. Look at the picture of Old Faithful. Explain what you know about Old Faithful. Draw a picture to answer the question.

Name: _____

Culture is the way people live.

This includes things like food, clothing, music, and art.

Culture

Time to Draw

Directions: Read about culture. Talk about what you see in the pictures. Draw something people do in your community. Tell about your picture.

Culture

Name: _____

Nature is the world around us that is not made by people.

Time to Draw

Nature Where I Live

Directions: Read about nature. Look at the pictures of nature. Talk about what you see. Draw nature in your community. Tell about your picture.

Name: _____

We change nature to help people.

This is the Golden Gate Bridge.

1	2	3	4	5
red	tan	blue	light blue	gray

Directions: Read about nature. Look at the example of how people change nature. Use the color code to color the Golden Gate Bridge. Talk about how this bridge changes nature and helps people.

Name: _____

People must take care of nature.

Time to Draw

Nature is fragile.

That means it can be hurt or broken.

I take care of nature.

Directions: Read the sentence. Look at the examples of people taking care of nature. Read about nature being fragile. Draw a picture about taking care of nature. Tell about your picture.

Culture

Name: _____

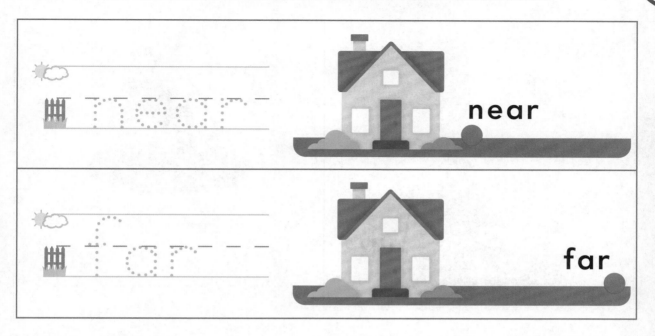

near

far

near	far

Directions: Trace the words *near* and *far*. Look at the examples of near and far. Talk about what you see. Draw something that is near you and something that is far from you. Tell about your pictures.

Name: _____

Maps and Geography

up	down

Directions: Trace the words *up* and *down*. Look at the examples of up and down. Talk about what you see. Draw something that is up and something that is down. Tell about your pictures. Act out being up and down.

Name: _____

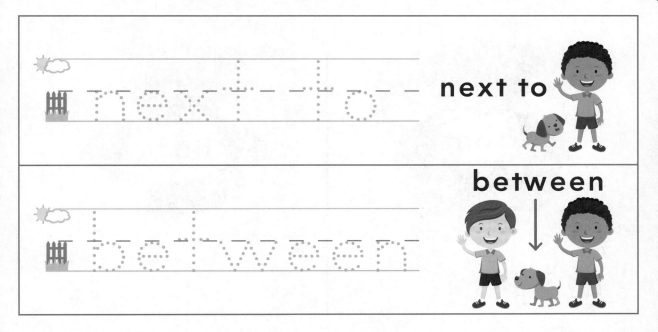

next to	between

Directions: Trace the words *next to* and *between*. Look at the examples of being next to and between. Talk about what you see. Draw something that is next to something else. Draw something that is between two things. Tell about your pictures. Act out being next to and between things.

Name: _____

Directions: Trace the words *front* and *back*. Look at the examples of front and back. Talk about what you see. Draw lines to match the fronts and backs of the objects in the pictures. Show front and back with objects around you.

left

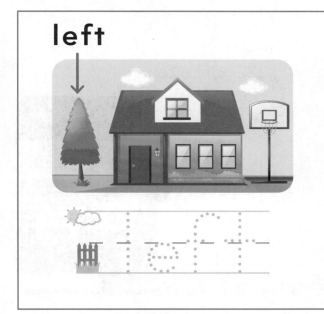

right

left and right

Directions: Trace the words *left* and *right*. Look at the examples of left and right. Draw a picture with two objects next to each other. Tell about your picture. Point to the object on the left and the object on the right.

Name: _____

Maps and Geography

 straight

Time to Draw

straight to...

Directions: Trace the word *straight* and the straight path. Talk about what you see. Then, draw lines to show the child walking straight to three places on the playground. Color the picture. Act out walking straight to places around the room.

Name: _____

A mountain is land that rises high above the places around it.

A forest is land that is mostly covered with trees.

Time to Draw

mountain	forest

Directions: Read about mountains and forests. Look at the example of a mountain and a forest. Talk about what you see. Draw a mountain and a forest. Talk about what you would like to do on a mountain or in a forest.

Maps and Geography

Name: _____

A canyon is a deep valley with tall sides.
A cliff is a tall rock face.

canyon

cliff

Time to Draw

canyon and cliff

Directions: Read about canyons and cliffs. Look at the examples of canyons and cliffs. Talk about what you see in the pictures. Draw a canyon and a cliff. Talk about the differences between a canyon and a cliff.

Name: _____

A prairie is land that is covered with grasses.

Farms may be on the prairie.

Prairie dogs live there.

prairie

prairie dog

Directions: Read about prairies. Color the example of a prairie. Talk about what you see in the pictures. Connect the dots to draw a prairie dog.

Name: _____

A desert is land that is very dry.
Deserts get very little rain.

Directions: Read about deserts. Color the example of a desert. Talk about what you see in the pictures. Talk about what animal you might like to see in a desert.

Name: _____

An island is land that has water all around it.

A beach is land with sand or rocks by the water.

island ————  ———— beach

Time to Draw

island	beach

Directions: Read about islands and beaches. Talk about what you see in the pictures. Color the example of an island. Draw a beach. Talk about what you would like to do on an island or a beach.

Name: _____

Maps and Geography

An ocean is a large body of salt water.

A river is a large stream of fresh water.

A lake is a large body of fresh water that has land all around it.

Time to Draw

ocean	river	lake

Directions: Read about oceans, rivers, and lakes. Explain what you see in the pictures. Draw pictures of an ocean, a river, and a lake. Tell about your pictures.

Name: _____

A map is a flat drawing of all or part of Earth.

A globe is a round map of Earth.

map

globe

Time to Draw

map and globe

m	a	p	b	c
d	l	m	a	p
i	j	k	o	d
m	a	p	t	n
o	m	a	p	r

Directions: Read about maps and globes. Talk about what you see in the examples. Draw a map and a globe. Tell about your pictures. Then, circle the word *map* four times in the word search.

Maps and Geography

Name: _____

A compass rose shows directions on a map.

It shows north, south, east, and west.

Directions: Read about a compass rose. Label your own compass rose. Talk about where north, south, east, and west are. Look around the room you're in. Use a cell phone or a map to figure out which way is north. Label the four walls with the directions.

Name: _____

A map key shows what the symbols on a map mean.

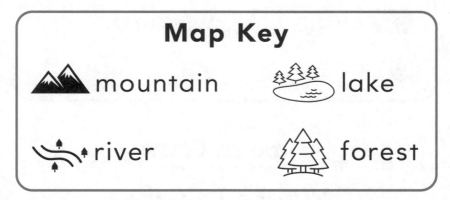

Map Key

🏔 mountain   🌲 lake

〰 river   🌲🌲 forest

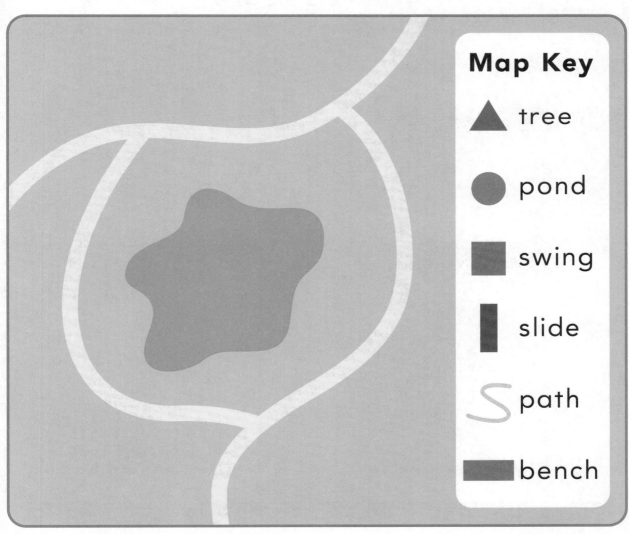

Map Key

▲ tree

● pond

■ swing

▮ slide

∫ path

▬ bench

Directions: Read about map keys. Talk about the example of a map key. Create your own map by drawing the symbols on the map. Share your map.

Name: _____

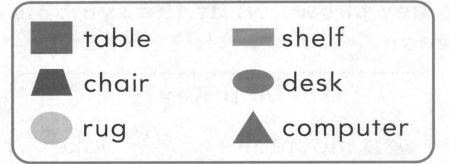

table	shelf
chair	desk
rug	computer

Time to Draw

Where I Learn

Directions: Use the map key to draw a map of where you learn. Color the symbols on the map according to the key. You may add more symbols to the key if you want. Tell about the symbols on the key and show where they are on the map.

Name: _____

Time to Draw

This sign means
stop.

stop

go

stop

go

Directions: Read about stop signs. Draw a red stop sign. Explain what you know about stop signs. Draw lines from the words *stop* and *go* to the pictures of stop signs and go signals.

Signs and Symbols

Name: _____

A yield sign means slow down and let others go first.

Time to Draw

Directions: Read about yield signs. Look at the examples of yield signs. Talk about what you see. Draw a place where you might see a yield sign. Share your picture. Practice yielding with a friend.

Name: _____

Caution means to be very careful.

Do not enter means not to go into an area.

Time to Draw

Directions: Read about these street signs. Talk about these signs. Draw a place where you might see these signs. Be sure to show one of the signs in your picture. Act out what you would do if you saw one of these signs.

Name: _____

These signs show where people may ride bikes.

Directions: Read about bike path signs. Look at the examples of bike path signs. Explain what you see in these signs. Trace the bike symbol. Circle three examples of bike path signs.

Name: _____

These signs mean there is a restroom.

A restroom is a bathroom.

Time to Draw

Directions: Read about restroom signs. Look at the examples of restroom signs. Talk about what you see. Draw a place where you might see a restroom sign. Share your picture.

Name: _____

This is a traffic signal.

red—Stop.

yellow—Get ready to stop.

green—Go.

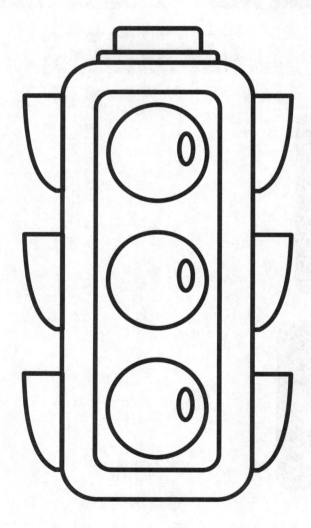

Signs and Symbols

Directions: Read about traffic signals. Explain what you know about these signs and lights. Color the traffic light. Play the game Red Light, Green Light.

Name: _____

These signs mean that a railroad crossing is ahead.

This light tells drivers to stop for a train.

1. Which shows a railroad crossing sign?

2. Which shows a railroad crossing light?

Directions: Read about railroad crossing signs and lights. Talk about being safe around railroads. Circle the best answers to the questions.

Name: _____

These signs show that people may cross the street.

These signs show when to cross the street and when not to.

Crosswalk Signs and Lights

Directions: Read about crosswalk signs and lights. Tell an adult what you know about crosswalk signs and lights. Color the pictures of a crosswalk sign and light.

Signs and Symbols

Name: _____

These signs show that animals may cross the road.

Time to Draw

Animal Crossing Signs

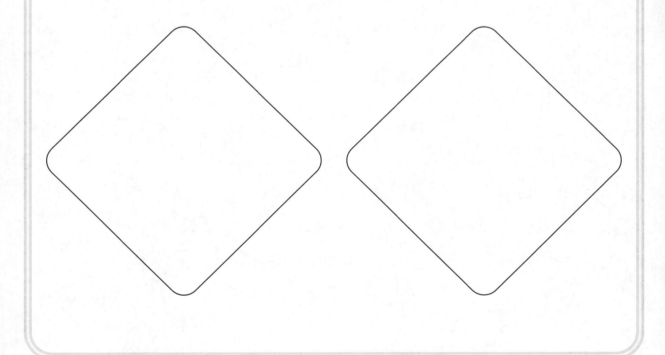

Directions: Read about animal crossing signs. Look at the examples. Talk about animal crossings. Draw two animal crossing signs of your own. Share your signs.

Name: _____

These signs tell that a playground is ahead.

STOP	traffic light	SLOW CHILDREN	restroom	CAUTION
red	orange	yellow	blue	green

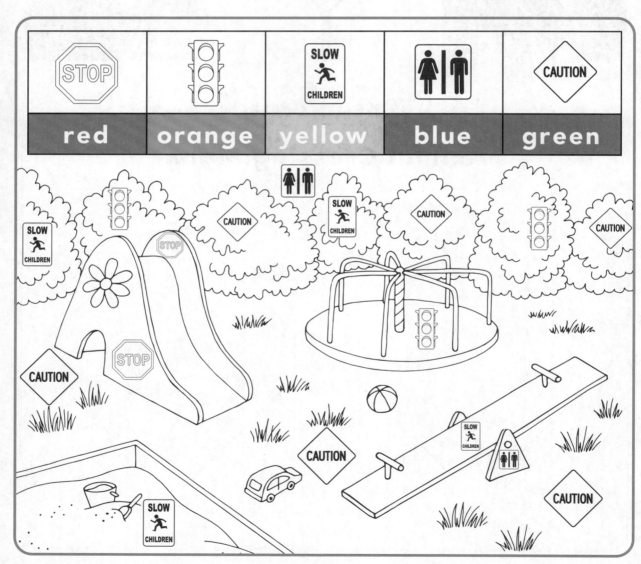

Directions: Read about and look at the playground signs. Explain what you know about playground signs and where you might see them. Use the color code to color the picture.

Name: _____

Sunny weather looks like this.

Time to Draw

Sunny Weather

Directions: Read the sentence. Talk about what you see in the pictures of sunny weather. Draw a sunny day where you live. Talk about your picture and how you feel on sunny days. Circle the pictures of sunny days.

Name: _____

Cloudy weather looks like this.

Time to Draw

Cloudy Weather

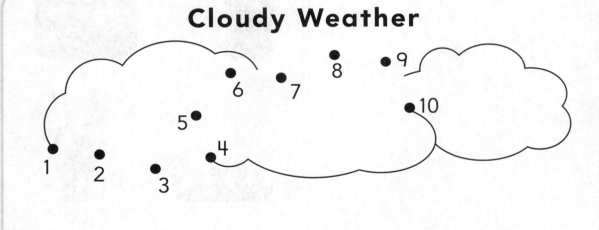

Directions: Trace the word *cloudy*. Talk about what you see in the examples of cloudy weather. Connect the dots to make clouds. Draw a picture below the clouds. Talk about your picture and how you feel on cloudy days.

Name: _____

 weather looks like this.

How People Live

Time to Draw

Directions: Trace the word *rainy*. Look at the pictures of rainy days. Talk about what you see in the examples of rainy weather. Draw a rainy day where you live. Talk about your picture and how you feel on rainy days.

Name: _____

How People Live

Snowy weather looks like this.

Time to Draw

Directions: Trace the word *snowy*. Look at the examples of snowy weather. Talk about what you see in the examples of snowy weather. Draw a snowy day. Talk about your picture and how you feel on snowy days. If you have never had a snowy day, imagine how it might feel.

Name: _____

Windy weather looks like this.

Directions: Read the sentence. Talk about what you see in the examples of windy weather. Put the pictures that tell a story about a windy day in order by writing 1, 2, and 3.

Name: _____

The weather can look like this during the seasons.

The seasons are spring, summer, fall, and winter.

Seasonal Weather

spring	summer
fall	winter

Directions: Read about seasons. Talk about what you know about seasons. Draw what the weather looks like in each season. Talk about your pictures and how they are different from one another.

Name: _____

People wear different clothing during each season.

Weather and Clothing	
cloudy spring day	sunny summer day
rainy fall day	snowy winter day

Directions: Read about clothing. Look at the examples of clothes people wear during the seasons. Draw clothes to wear during each type of day. Tell about your pictures.

Name: _____

People like to eat special foods during each season.

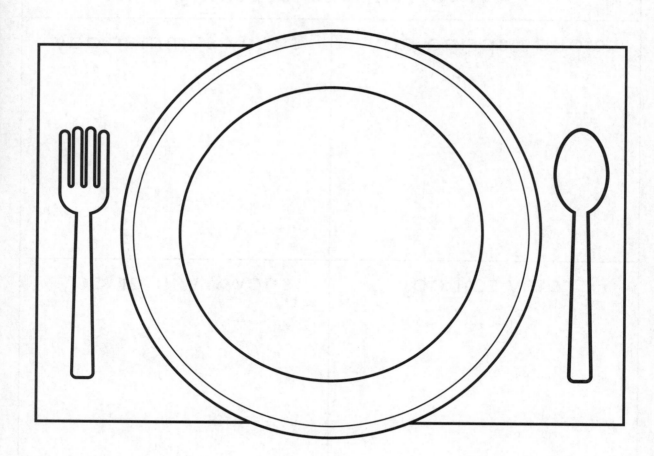

Directions: Read about special foods. Talk about what you see in the pictures. Draw a special food you like to eat during one of the seasons. Tell about your picture.

130220—180 Days of Social Studies for Prekindergarten

© Shell Education

Name: _____

The weather changes during the seasons.

People do different things at home when the weather changes.

Seasons at Home	
cloudy spring day	sunny summer day
rainy fall day	snowy winter day

Directions: Read about what people do in different seasons. Talk about what you see in the pictures. Draw a home during each type of day. Tell about your pictures.

Name: _____

People do outdoor activities.

The activities can change with the weather.

Weather and Outdoor Activities	
cloudy spring day	sunny summer day
rainy fall day	snowy winter day

Directions: Read about outdoor activities. Talk about what you see in the pictures. Draw outdoor activities you can do during each season. Tell about your pictures. Act out the activities.

Name: _____

When you own something, it belongs to you or your family.

Time to Draw

What belongs to you?
What belongs to your family?

Directions: Read about owning things. Look at the examples of things people own. Read the questions. Talk about what you own and what your family owns. Draw something you own. Draw something your family owns. Tell about your pictures.

Name: _____

Choices

Sharing means giving someone part of something.

Time to Draw

Directions: Read about and trace the word *sharing*. Talk about what you see in the pictures. Draw yourself sharing with someone. Act out your picture.

130220—180 Days of Social Studies for Prekindergarten

© Shell Education

We make choices.

Our choices affect others.

Choices

Choices	How do others feel?
A child buys the last candy.	
The children share the pizza.	

Directions: Read about making choices. Talk about what you see in the pictures. Color the picture showing how choices can make others feel. Finish the face to show how the children who share the pizza feel.

Name: _____

Sometimes, there is not enough of something.

We have to choose something else.

Choosing Something Else

Directions: Read about making choices. Look at the pictures. Talk about what you see. Color the example. Circle examples of making choices when there is not enough. Act out one of the examples.

We Make Choices

1 cent

2 cents

5 cents

Time to Draw

Directions: Talk about the candy you would choose to buy from the candy machine and why you would choose it. Circle the candy you would choose. How much would the candy cost? Draw you or your family choosing something to buy at a store. Tell about your picture.

Choices

Name: _____

Making Choices

give

get

Directions: Trace the words *give* and *get*. Color the pictures. Talk about what the boy is giving up and what he is getting.

Name: _____

Making Choices

Directions: Read about making choices. Talk about the way you and your family make choices when you are choosing what to buy. Color the example. Circle one toy you would buy with $1.00. Explain why you chose that toy.

Name: _____

Choices

Time to Draw

I make choices.

1	2	3	4
yellow	pink	blue	brown

Directions: Talk about how you make choices with money. Draw how you keep (or would keep) your money in a safe place. Tell about your picture. Use the color code to color the picture.

Name: _____

Producers make things that people buy.

Time to Draw

Directions: Read about producers. Look at the pictures. Talk about what you see. Draw a producer making something that your family buys. Tell about your picture.

Goods and Services

Name: _____

Consumers are people who buy things.

 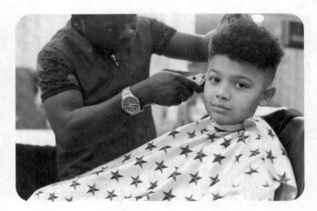

1. Who is a consumer?

2. Who is a producer?

Directions: Read about consumers. Look at the examples of consumers. Talk about what you see in the pictures. Circle the pictures that show a consumer and a producer.

Name: _____

Goods are things that are made or grown.

People can buy goods.

Goods can be touched.

Goods That Are Made	Goods That Are Grown

Directions: Read about goods. Look at the examples of goods. Talk about goods that are made and goods that are grown. Draw goods that are made and goods that are grown. Tell about your pictures.

Name: _____

Goods have different values.

Value means how much something is worth.

$1.00

$3.00

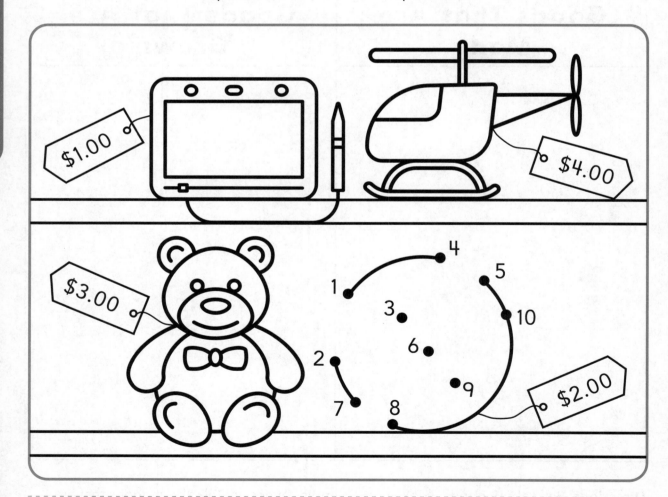

Directions: Read about the values of goods. Talk about how goods have different values. Connect the dots, and color the pictures. Which of these goods might you like to buy?

Name: _____

A  service is a job you pay someone else to do.

Goods and Services

Time to Draw

Directions: Read about and trace the word *service*. Look at the examples of services. Talk about services that you and your family pay someone else to do. Draw a picture of a service in your community. Act out doing this service.

Name: _____

Goods are objects that are made or grown.

Goods are things you can touch.

Services are jobs we pay other people to do.

Is it a good or service?

pet grooming

driving a bus

fixing a car

Directions: Read about goods and services. Look at the examples of goods and services. Circle the goods in red. Circle the services in blue. Talk about goods and services that you and your family use.

Name: _____

Resources are things we use to make goods and give services.

A doctor is a resource.

Water is a resource.

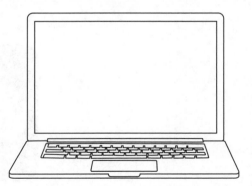

A computer is a resource.

Directions: Read about resources. Look at the examples of resources. Talk about how these resources are used for goods and services. Color the pictures.

Name: _____

Computers are goods we can buy.

They also help us get services.

Directions: Read about computers. Look at the examples of computers. Talk about the services we can get from computers. Draw lines to match the computers with the services. Talk about services.

Goods or Services?

baker

babysitter

window washer

loaf of bread

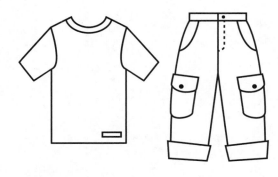

shirt and pants

soccer ball

Directions: Look at the examples of goods and services. Circle the goods, and draw a line under the services. Color the examples. Explain what you know about the services. Pretend that you are buying the goods at a store.

Name: _____

A market is a place where people buy and sell goods and services.

One kind of market is called a store.

Time to Draw

Directions: Read about markets. Look at the examples of markets. Talk about markets in your community. Imagine that you own a market. Draw products you would sell at your market. Tell about your pictures.

The goods and services we buy have prices.

The prices are how much money they cost to buy.

5 dollars

Prices

What is the price of this pen?

$ _____

Directions: Read about prices. Look at the examples. Talk about the prices of goods and services. Read the speech bubble. Write how much you think the pen would cost.

Name: _____

Some goods are made or grown in our community.

They are local.

Some are made or grown in other places.

Directions: Read about local goods. Look at the examples of local goods. Talk about local goods near you. Write 1, 2, and 3 to put the pictures showing doughnuts being made in order. Talk about bakeries in your community.

Name: _____

Trading is one way to get goods.

Trading means giving something to get something.

Time to Draw

How do I trade goods?

Directions: Read about trading goods. Look at the example of trading goods. Talk about trading goods. Read the question. Draw yourself trading goods. Tell about your picture. Act out trading.

Name: _____

Trading is one way to get services.

Trading means giving something to get something.

Trading Services

Directions: Read about trading services. Look at the example of trading services. Talk about trading services. Look at the examples of trading. Circle the example that shows trading services. Act out the example of trading services.

Name: _____

Trading and buying are both ways to get goods.

trading

buying

trading

buying

Directions: Read the sentence. Talk about how buying and trading are different. Draw lines from the words to the pictures that match.

Name: _____

Money and Jobs

Money is what people use to buy goods and services.

Time to Draw

What do I know about money?

Directions: Read about money. Talk about how you use money. Look at the examples of money. Draw a picture about money. Act out using money to buy something.

Name: _____

A coin is a piece of metal money that is small, flat, and round.

Coins

Directions: Read about coins. Look at the examples of coins. Talk about them. Circle and color the coins. Talk about the names of the coins.

Name: _____

 **are paper money.**

Time to Draw

What do I know about bills?

Directions: Read about and trace the word *bills*. Look at the examples of bills. Talk about bills you have seen. Draw a picture about bills. Tell about your picture. Act out using paper money to buy or sell goods.

Name: _____

Jobs are work that people do to earn money.

1. Who is a firefighter on the job?

2. Who is a farmer on the job?

Directions: Read about jobs. Look at the examples of jobs. Talk about jobs you know. Circle the pictures that show a firefighter and a farmer. Act out a job you would like to do.

Name: _____

Job	What They Do
baker	
bus driver	
builder	

Directions: Look at the examples of jobs. Talk about these three jobs. Draw what a baker, bus driver, and builder do. Tell about your pictures. Act out one of these jobs.

Name: _____

Jobs are work that people do to earn money.

People can use the money to buy goods or services.

I can buy it now!

Directions: Read about jobs and money. Talk about how people earn money working at a job. Put the story about earning and spending money in order by writing 1, 2, and 3. Act out earning money and buying something you want.

Money and Jobs

Name: _____

I buy the game.	I earn and save money.	I want the game.

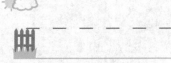		

Time to Draw

Directions: With an adult, read the story about getting a game. Write 1, 2, and 3 to put the story in the correct order. Draw something you would like to buy. Tell about your drawing.

Name: _____

Needs are things that people must have to live.

Basic needs are food, water, shelter, and clothing.

food   water   shelter   clothing

Time to Draw

Needs and Wants

Directions: Read about needs. Talk about your basic needs. Trace the word *needs*. Draw your basic needs. Share your picture.

Needs and Wants

Name: _____

Needs are things that people must have to live.

Basic needs are food, water, shelter, and clothing.

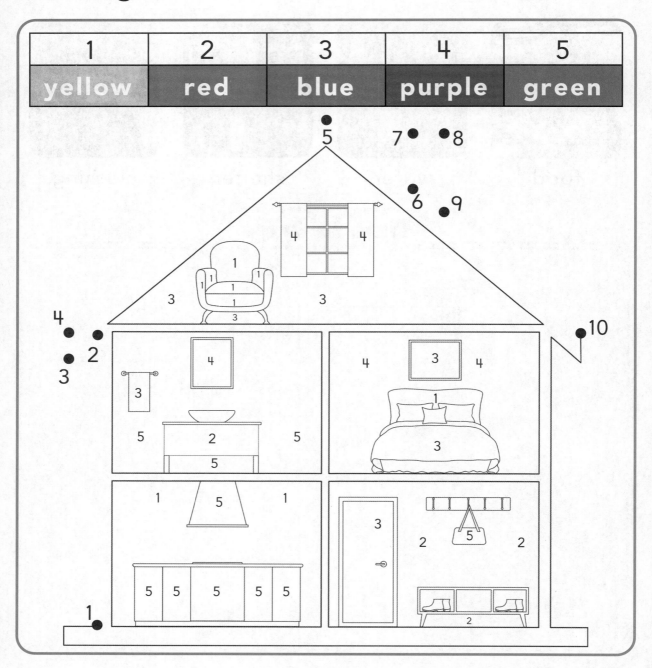

1	2	3	4	5
yellow	red	blue	purple	green

Directions: Read about needs. Talk about your basic needs. Connect the dots to make a picture of one of the basic needs. Color the picture using the color code.

130220—180 Days of Social Studies for Prekindergarten

Name: _____

We can make choices about the needs we buy.

She likes this kind of cereal.

c	n	e	e	d
n	n	e	e	d	l
d	d	n	e	e	d
f	g	u	s	m
n	n	e	e	d	o

Needs and Wants

Time to Draw

Directions: Read about buying things you need. Look at the example. Talk about why cereal is a need. Draw the kinds of foods your family buys. Then, circle the word *need* four times in the word search.

Name: _____

Wants are things a person would like to have.

Needs and Wants

Time to Draw

wants

Directions: Read about wants. Talk about things you want. Trace the word *wants*. Draw things you want. Tell about your picture.

Wants Where I Learn

w	a	n	t	e
c	w	a	n	t
d	f	o	p	l
w	a	n	t	f
g	w	a	n	t

Directions: Look at the examples of things students might want where they learn. Talk about what you want for the place where you learn. Draw these things. Share your picture. Then, circle the word *want* four times in the word search.

Name: _____

We want a lot of things.

People want more goods.

People cannot have everything they want.

Directions: Read about wanting more. Talk about wanting more. Look at the three examples of why we cannot always have more. Circle the picture that shows what you want more of.

Needs and Wants

Buying something you want.

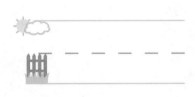

Directions: Look at the examples of needs and wants. Talk about needs and wants. Circle the needs in red and the wants in blue. Put the story of someone buying what they want in order by writing 1, 2, and 3. Tell the story that the pictures show.

Name: _____

Needs and Wants

Time to Draw

Family Needs

Time to Draw

Family Wants

Directions: Talk about things a family might need and want. Draw what you think your family needs. Then, draw what you think your family wants. Share your pictures.

Name: _____

Something is scarce if there is not a lot of it.

Needs and Wants

The lemonade is scarce.

Directions: Read about what scarce means. Practice saying the word *scarce*. Look at the pictures of the lemonade that is scarce. Tell the story about the pictures in your own words. Explain what you would do to solve the problem if this were your lemonade stand.

Name: _____

Our wants and needs change as we grow.

Needs and Wants

Baby	Today

Directions: Read about change. Talk about what your wants and needs were as a baby. Draw your wants and needs as a baby. Then, draw your wants and needs today. Share your pictures.

Congratulations!
You did it!

Congratulations to:

_____

Achievement:

You worked hard for 180 days to learn social studies!

Way to go! You did your best!

Awarded by: _____ **Date:** _____

Directions: Read each word aloud with an adult. Draw yourself learning about social studies. Post this certificate somewhere special.

Rubric

Directions: This rubric can be used for any open-ended questions where student responses vary. Evaluate student work to determine how many points out of 9 students earn. Discuss answers with the child to ensure understanding. It is developmentally appropriate for children at this level to express ideas with drawings only. In these cases, discuss the child's drawings.

Student Name: _____

	3 Points	2 Points	1 Point
Content Knowledge	Gives right answer based on content *and* prior knowledge.	Gives right or mostly right answer based on content *or* prior knowledge.	Gives incorrect answer.
Analysis	Thinks about the content and draws correct and strong inferences/conclusions.	Thinks about the content and draws somewhat correct inferences/conclusions.	Thinks about the content but draws incorrect inferences/conclusions.
Explanation	Explains and supports responses with robust evidence.	Explains and supports responses with some evidence.	Provides little or no evidence for responses.

Total: _____

_____

_____

_____

_____

_____

_____

Semester Recording Sheet

Directions: Select days at the beginning and end of each semester to use the Rubric (page 196) to score students' responses. After scoring, record students' scores here. Compare the two scores each semester.

	Student Name	S1 Date	S1 Date	S2 Date	S2 Date
1.					
2.					
3.					
4.					
5.					
6.					
7.					
8.					
9.					
10.					
11.					
12.					
13.					
14.					
15.					
16.					
17.					
18.					
19.					
20.					

Trimester Recording Sheet

Directions: Select days at the beginning and end of each trimester to use the Rubric (page 196) to score students' responses. After scoring, record students' scores here. Compare the two scores each trimester.

	Student Name	T1 Date	T1 Date	T2 Date	T2 Date	T3 Date	T3 Date
1.							
2.							
3.							
4.							
5.							
6.							
7.							
8.							
9.							
10.							
11.							
12.							
13.							
14.							
15.							
16.							
17.							
18.							
19.							
20.							

Four Disciplines Recording Sheet

Directions: At the beginning and end of each of the four disciplines of this book, use the Rubric (page 196) to score students' responses. After scoring, record students' scores here. Compare the two scores for each of the four disciplines.

	Student Name	History Date	History Date	Civics Date	Civics Date	Geography Date	Geography Date	Economics Date	Economics Date
1.									
2.									
3.									
4.									
5.									
6.									
7.									
8.									
9.									
10.									
11.									
12.									
13.									
14.									
15.									
16.									
17.									
18.									
19.									
20.									

References Cited

Byington, Teresa A., and Y. Kim. 2017. "Promoting Preschoolers' Emergent Writing." *Young Children* 72 (5). www.naeyc.org/resources/pubs/yc/nov2017/emergent-writing.

Durden, Tonia, Elsa Lucia Escalante-Barrios, and Kimberly Blitch. 2015. "Start with Us! Culturally Relevant Pedagogy in the Preschool Classroom." *Early Childhood Education Journal* 43 (3), 223–232.

First Things First. 2017. "Early Childhood Brain Development Has Lifelong Impact." *Arizona PBS*. azpbs.org/2017/11/early-childhood-brain-development-lifelong-impact.

Gay, Geneva. 2000. *Culturally Responsive Teaching: Theory, Research, and Practice.* New York: Teachers College Press.

Goodman, Kela, and Laura Hooks. 2016. "Encouraging Family Involvement through Culturally Relevant Pedagogy." *SRATE Journal* 25 (2), 33–41.

Hirsch, Megan. 2010. *How to Hold a Pencil.* Los Angeles, CA: Hirsch Indie Press.

Ladson-Billings, Gloria. 1995. "But That's Just Good Teaching! The Case for Culturally Relevant Pedagogy." *Theory into Practice* 34 (3), 159–165.

National Council for the Social Studies (NCSS). 2010. *National Curriculum Standards for Social Studies: A Framework for Teaching, Learning, and Assessment.* Silver Spring, MD: National Council for the Social Studies.

———. 2013. *The College, Career, and Civic Life (C3) Framework for Social Studies State Standards: Guidance for Enhancing the Rigor of K-12 Civics, Economics, Geography, and History.* Silver Spring, MD: National Council for the Social Studies.

Strasser, Janis., and Lisa Mufson Bresson. 2017. *Big Questions for Young Minds: Extending Children's Thinking.* Washington, DC: National Association for the Education of Young Children.

Answer Key

page 21

1. Which is a cold winter day?

2. Which should you wear on a cold winter day?

page 23

page 27
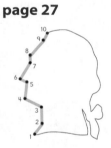

page 28
Plant a Tree

page 31
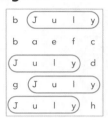

page 33

page 35
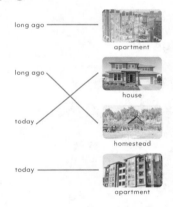

page 38

page 41
1. Which shows a way to make light today?
2. Which shows a way to make light long ago?

page 44
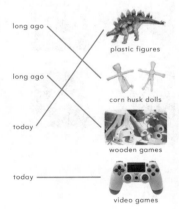

Answer Key *(cont.)*

page 46

page 66

page 70

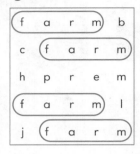

page 52

page 68

Students should draw tools that lifeguards use, such as floats, binoculars, whistles, lifeguard uniform, and sunscreen next to the megaphone.

page 73

Students should color the utility workers' tools and draw one more: screwdriver, hammer, hard hat, gloves, etc.

page 74

Students should color the custodians' tools and draw more: sprays, towels, vacuum cleaners, brooms, etc.

page 58

page 69

page 77

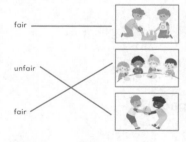

page 60

Answer Key (cont.)

page 79

page 86

page 95

page 81

page 92

page 82

page 97

page 94

page 83

page 98

Answer Key *(cont.)*

page 99

page 102

page 106

page 107

page 108

page 110

page 111

b	j	A	b	e
b	a	l	m	n
A	b	e	y	d
g	k	A	b	e
A	b	e	q	t

page 117

page 122

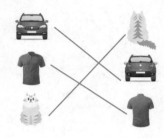

page 124

Students should draw three straight lines from the child on the playground to three places on the playground.

page 127

page 131

m	a	p	b	c
d	l	m	a	p
i	j	k	o	d
m	a	p	t	n
o	m	a	p	r

Answer Key *(cont.)*

page 133

Students should use the given symbols on the map key to draw on the map to make a playground.

page 134

Students should use the given symbols on the map key to make a map of where they learn.

page 135

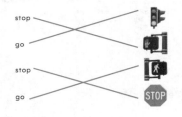

page 138

page 141

1. Which shows a railroad crossing sign?

2. Which shows a railroad crossing light?

page 144

page 145

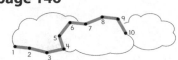

page 146

page 149

page 158

page 159

Students should circle the candy machine they would buy from.

page 161

Students should circle the toy they would buy with $1.00.

page 162

page 164

1. Who is a consumer?

2. Who is a producer?

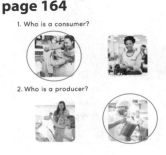

Answer Key *(cont.)*

page 166

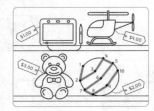

page 174

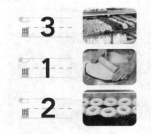

page 183

page 168

page 176

page 184

page 170

page 177

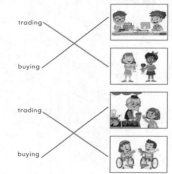

page 186

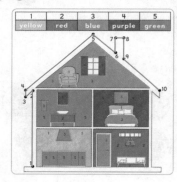

page 171

page 181

page 187

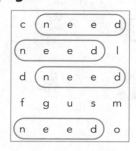

Answer Key *(cont.)*

page 189

w	a	n	t	e
c	w	a	n	t
d	f	o	p	l
w	a	n	t	f
g	w	a	n	t

page 191

1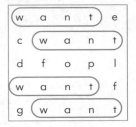

2

3

Digital Resources

Accessing the Digital Resources

The digital resources can be downloaded by following these steps:

1. Go to **www.tcmpub.com/digital**

2. Use the ISBN number to redeem the digital resources.

3. Respond to the question using the book.

4. Follow the prompts on the Content Cloud website to sign in or create a new account.

5. The content redeemed will now be on your My Content screen. Click on the product to look through the digital resources. All resources are available for download. Select files can be previewed, opened, and shared.

   For questions and assistance with your license key card, or to report a lost card, please contact Shell Education.

   email: customerservice@tcmpub.com
   phone: 800-858-7339

Contents of the Digital Resources

Activities

- Ideas for extending the learning to real-world situations

- Community Helpers Matching Game

- Templates for creating student books about social studies topics

- Hands-on practice for learning uppercase and lowercase letters

- Writing practice of uppercase and lowercase letters

Teacher Resources

- Certificate of Completion

- Rubric

- Recording Sheets

- Standards Correlations